Tentmaking

By Coleman Barks

POETRY

The Juice

New Words

We're Laughing at the Damage

Gourd Seed

TRANSLATIONS

Rumi

Night and Sleep

Open Secret

Unseen Rain

We Are Three

These Branching Moments

This Longing

Delicious Laughter

Like This

Feeling the Shoulder of the Lion

Birdsong

The Hand of Poetry

Say I Am You

The Essential Rumi

The Illuminated Rumi

The Glance

The Soul of Rumi

6th Dalai Lama

Stallion on a Frozen Lake

Lalla

Naked Song

Coleman Barks

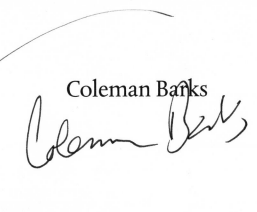

Tentmaking

POEMS AND PROSE PARAGRAPHS

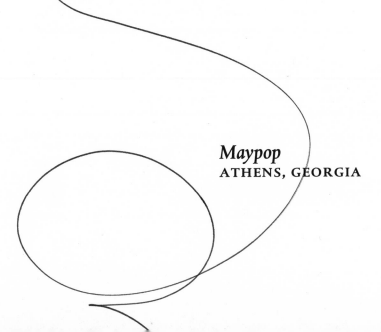

Maypop
ATHENS, GEORGIA

Maypop Books
196 Westview Dr.
Athens, GA 30606

800-682-8637

maypopbooks.com

ISBN - 1-884237-02-9

Some of these were previously published in the following: *Georgia Review, Seneca Review, Smartish Pace, Solo, The Blue Sofa Review, Verse, Figdust,* the Whole Life internet site, *The North Stone Review, Courtland Review, Nightsun, Texas Review, The Best American Poetry 1999, Ann Arbor Review* and *Rivendell.*

for John Seawright

CONTENTS

Tentmaking

Bill Pettway came to visit the other night,
    and there were four walls of water pouring
        down into a square cistern where he was showing

me how our lives are one volume in constant
    revision, language being always altered, and how
        revisions overlap and duplicate

each other, as some revisions I was bringing were already
    being made. Then the realization in the dream
        that Pettway was dead. He died suddenly

several years ago heaving lumber into the back of a truck.
    My memories of him go back to kindergarten when
        he did the most daring criminal act

anyone ever considered: he threw scissors off the balcony
    where some were doing art down into the area
        where the rest of us were.

I imagine he remembers doing that in the place he comes
    to my dreams from. Now the maroon squares
        of the kindergarten floor come

clear, where cots were put out for our afternoon naps,
    and this: I slept longer and deeper than
        anyone, and the wonder is they

let me: each afternoon to wake and be the only cot
    there in the big room. Maybe the janitor
        would still be carrying and stacking the canvas

cots in the hall or maybe he had finished and gone.
    That aloneness stays inside me like an afternoon.
        Like summer turning night and lightning

bugs, their beauty floating my height in a hollow of
    black locust, oak, and hickory, some higher
        in the branches. The point is not to put them

in a jar where they clump and quit winking and next
        morning smell of exhausted phosphor.
                Leave the lovers of scintillae in the air

they love, gracing distance with their dance. Pettway
        was telling me that every moment contains the dead
                and they are not dead, but doing

this revision with us. And that I should get my
        revisions out *quicker*. I was keeping
                them in my mind too long. At the end he began

speaking a Borneo dialect, which appeared in script to
        the side, *Oolek bineng weresak*, not
                that exactly but similiar. And the next night new

Ohio poems by James Wright came, a canoe seen from above, the
        line of its motion in the river behind it
                briefly. Wright and Bly were helping me teach

a poetry class. Pettway was there with his mouth open in an O.
        His nickname through high school was Puss.
                He dated Jean Carter, whose pale and freckled red-headed

body kindled my desire for women early on the bank of
        Chickamauga Lake lying under the full moon pouring its
                wrinkling waterpath to us. Then the freckling on

her legs in dream became a vine design one could somehow drink
        and slake desire for those legs, for a time.
                Time and time words build their contradiction. Call it

tentmaking: one twists rope; another carves wooden pegs; someone
        weaves; there's a man stitching and one tearing
                cloth. Reprobate and righteous,

loyal, dis; provoker and provoked. We cannot help but do this we
        are. This *is*, and even if we could see
                the purpose, still no one's faith would increase. Every

act is praise, no matter. I know a man who was standing in a long
    line for a movie with a huge amount of
        coins in his pockets, hundreds of dimes, nickels,

quarters, pennies. He suddenly spills all to the sidewalk and
    changes everything: stiff and separate
        people bend and gather, helping, laughing, stealing; they

throw handfuls into the grassy medians of the parking lot; saying
    becomes rolling coinage. We are nothing
        but some seeing that includes those who have died:

desire and collective editing: a wooden truckload, this river of
    roots where a golden-legged lover builds a tent
        of cover and her body over me. We

talk inside this word-wet hearing-fog we breathe.

Purring

The internet says science is not sure how cats purr,
  probably a vibration of the whole
      larynx, unlike what we do when we talk. Less

likely, a blood vessel moving across the chest wall.
  As a child I tried to make every
      cat I met purr. That was one of the early

miracles, the stroking to perfection. Here's something
  I've never heard: a feline purrs in
      two conditions, when deeply content and when

mortally wounded, to calm themselves, readying for the
  death-opening. The low frequency
      evidently helps to strengthen bones and

heal damaged organs. Say poetry is a human purr, vessel
  mooring in the chest, a closed-mouth
      refuge, the feel of a glide through dying: one

winter morning on a sunny chair inside this only body,
  a faroff inboard motorboat sings
      the empty room, urrrrrrrrrrrrrrrrrrrhhhhhhhh

What's Enough

Is writing and reading enough for some people? They don't
    need to work on themselves with a
        psychoanalyst or meditate or go on pilgrimage

with an enlightened being, embodied or not? They read,
    and they write. No sufi shrine
        encampment, no waterfall discourse. A line from

a 10th century woman, *Moonlight leaks between the roof planks*
    of this ruined house, makes
        them weep, or they taste the mixed grace of

Twelfth Night ending, *A great while ago the world began with*
    hey, ho, the wind and the
        rain. Their crown chakras flicker to life like

sprinklers on a street at 4 a.m. Their rooms draped with
    open books, they have no way
        to make a living but to read outloud whatever

word-bunch astonishments they find to students, do that
    thirty years. That's what we
        want them to. The wordway is a steep pleasure

in elegant turns, a mouthopen thankfulness for what's put
    right, the truth of soulmaking,
        that leads to the compassionate attention to

what's in front of us breathing intelligence. I bow to
    the scruffy summernight
        bookstore wanderers, my friends. Nobody

says it, but surely the enlightened ones include *makers,*
    each unique in the high art of
        soul: Shakespeare, Whitman, Emily, Leo, Mirabai,

Kabir, van Gogh, Beethoven, Amadeus, David, Hafez, Mark Twain,
    Memling, Wordsworth,
        Yeats and Keats. Hopkins. Everyone's list

is different. Some have country music people, shoemakers,
        drunks, and carpenters. English
                teachers. Yet we agree. Cormac, Blake, Rilke,

Sophocles, Aligheri. I was talking last night with Pete,
        the son of a football coach from
                Macon. Pete loves all manner of book. Pete

says, "You know, we talk about the sacred nature of each
        day, and I nod, agreeing, but
                I don't really believe anything." I love his

effort to be clear and pure. I don't believe anything
        either. I stay open, but
                if I haven't had some experience of the invisible,

I keep quiet. I have never seen a ghost, a virgin birth, a
        UFO, or a crop circle forming
                in the night. Except in dream. In dream I have

felt how the world is saturated wet with love as midnight
        dew, and passing through
                those grasses, inspiration like a steady river

picturing the scurry and settling of wings and fin.

Divination

Our game is to lower a fluffing riffle of
    dictionary pages held
        dangling by the front and back covers, its

fingertip toeholds slowly up and down and across
    my erect penis pointing
        to the ceiling to see what word its tip

nudges into notice: *pathos!* The ache that suffers
    through the fingers, then
        pendulous. Your breasts take hold and words

go blurry inside the *smoor* of where they point.
    And I can't help claiming
        we have found a way to honor at one time

two loves, for language and for the body,
    though clearly more
        research is indicated.

Book Tour Cure for Talking Too Much in Public

Be met at the suite door, deprived of handheld items,
    discalced by one already kneeling, unsocked,
        your sweet-smelly feet caressed

and pinktoenailed toes cleaned in between with a wet
    cloth and tickled; arch, heel, and ankle
        footwashed like an early Christian. Now

sit and let your pants be pulled, shirt unbuttoned,
    bra and panties tossed into tomorrow.
        Diswrist watch, leaving only Kwan Yin at the

greenwhirling center, for I too am naked who
    lead you to the perfect shower and soap your
        Corinthian shoulders and breasts and knees

and neck and Cappadocian me and rub you Smyrna priestess
    dry and me and walk us tottering Mesopotamians
        to bed to schmooz and kiss and writhe

and curl inside the creamy filling. When time comes
    sliding back—a truck gears down outside—
        we'll go somewhere that's open and eat.

Question

I know that you love me. You
    love my eyes. You love my eyes
        looking in your eyes with our love,

and all. Sometimes you want to pound me with your tiny
    beautiful fists and your insistent,
        skinny, so-sensitive undersided, forearms.

This will all go away, my eyes,
    your skin, what we so love and the energy
        of their beauty, the parts.

My question is not when.
    Let that sequence be. I even claim that some
        of my love for you will go

right through the ornate wooden panel of dying.
    I feel the wholeness of it will.
        Oh I have no question. I thought I did,

but I don't. Do. You that love the erotic
    stars and paperclips, will I have
        to watch you making love with a man other than

me? Poor me. I watch you near me, in you, so sweetly.
    Will I have to hear your moans mix
        with another's mouth making the chorale

of spring? Will you have to hear mine? I feel sad
    asking this, but I do with some courage
        ask. And answer my side of it no and I don't

know. But living-hearing the synchronous
    music of this friendship is so much the ordinary
        air being breathed

it would feel unnatural not to be that word
    I have rarely used, faithful,
        yours. Peeper,

shall we consider unasked what never could be answered
    anyway? With poignant howl and under-grumble
        the sentimental nightly

train leaves empty: a light waggle
    to the line of cars is
        how I guess.

I love the tentative balance of this wild devotion,
    our urgent hungering with
        meditation, this evening walk I invite

you for. Notebooks handy to the sudden phrase, a
    green glove, your hand on my wrist.
        Tomorrow is Candlemas,

the day of the dead, how they stay and what they care
    about, no longer ask of, how they see and
        visit our shawl of silence

as a small wind spirals flame. Grateful
    for what's given, not always able to bear
        it, going out.

Basement Lounge

Around eight o'clock Kenneth Rexroth stands
    behind a grape crate lectern turned
        on its end. This is for a midget who's

going to read *The Iliad* in haiku form, he says.
    Then Allen Ginsberg reads *Howl.* Gary
        Snyder, Philip Whalen, McClure and Lamantia

also read that night, Oct. 13, 1955. The small San
    Francisco audience includes Kerouac, Corso,
        and Ferlinghetti. I am a freshman

in Room 227 of Cobb Dorm at UNC. About eleven
    eastern, eight Pacific, I go down to the basement
        lounge to read, so as not to keep my

roommate, Wilson Cooper, awake, Faulkner's *As I Lay*
    Dying. In my dream last night I'm giving a
        class lecture on Bergson's feel

for how duration accumulates, swells inside awareness,
    while succession plods along as inexorable
        fact and Faulkner's way of

telling a story that admits it can't be told, just briefly
    the candlelit increments of inner speech
        from the various family and wayside observers,

as the mother Addie lies in bed expiring, then borne
    on gruesome, silly, magnificent parade to her final filled-in
        hole, she with only one segment

to say her lovings and how she managed the school teaching,
    her affair with the preacher. So there I was
        silently mouthing in that flourescent

student lounge language for my own repressed sexual
    longing and how it feels to run and swim and ride
        and lean back in the mud of some moment.

Bill Matthews Coming Along

They say the best French wines have *terroir*, meaning the taste of the lay of the land that works through and gets held in the wine, the bouquet of a particular hillside and of the care of those who work there.

When I see Bill Matthews coming along, I see and taste the culture of the world, a lively city, a university campus during Christmas break, a few friendly straggling scholars and artists. I taste the delight of language and desire and music. I see a saint of the great impulse that takes us out at night, to the opera, to the ballgame, to a movie, to poetry, a bar of music, a bar of friends.

When I see Bill Matthews stopped at the end of a long hall, I see my soul waiting for me to catch up, patient, demanding, wanting truth no matter what, the goofiest joke, the work with words we're here to do, saying how it is with emptiness and changing love, and the unchanging. Now I see his two tall sons behind him.

Bill would not say it this way; he might even start softly humming *Amazing Grace* if I began my saying, but I go on anyway: god is little g, inside out, a transparency that drenches everything you help us notice: a red blouse, those black kids crossing Amsterdam, braving the cabs, a nun. You sweet theologian, you grew new names for god: gourmet, cleaning woman, jazz, spring snow.

What fineness and finesse. I love Bill Matthews, and I did not have near enough time walking along with him, talking books and ideas, or sitting down to drink the slant and tender face of Provence.

Black Rubber Ball

Late one Thursday afternoon I arrive in Vermont from Georgia. I have been invited to the Bennington campus to give three lectures on "The Nature and Uses of Ecstatic Poetry." That night I dream of people in south India throwing a ball back and forth across an amphitheatre with steep seats. They are very adept at throwing and catching a blue ball, smaller than a volley ball, larger than a softball.

I give my first lecture in a room with steep seats, and afterward talking on the phone with my friend Judith Orloff, I tell her the dream. She gets an intuitive hit that I should mention the word ball in my second lecture. "Promise me you will."

Walking the campus later, I think to buy a ball, but where, in the bookstore? Since I would be talking next about playfulness in poetry, I could toss it around and involve the audience. The sun was going down and the new moon coming up as that idea broke through at the top of a rise on the path to my guest house. It was the new moon signaling the end of Ramadan, a traditionally auspicious moment.

A few steps further on where the path dips beside a pond, I see a black rubber ball! Almost in the center of the walkway. I pick it up with amazed gratitude and put it to good use in the next lecture. It turns out an audience's attention sharpens considerably when there's the possibility a ball might be thrown to anyone at any moment.

I am surprised and honored to see Mary Oliver in the audience. She teaches part of the year at Bennington and to my mind is the greatest living ecstatic poet. She comes up and pulls on my sleeve, "I left that ball for you." She was walking her dogs, Ben and Bear, and left that black rubber ball behind. It wasn't her dogs' toy. She saw it over in the grass and brought it to the path for whoever might come by.

All this, before I had the idea. She didn't have me especially in mind, but I was chosen, blackballed! And now I use this Greek instrument for ostracizing to show how playfully intelligent the web of connections is we live. The 13th century mystic Rumi says form itself is ecstatic: being shaped and sentient a state of pure rapture.

Follow the bouncing ball and sing along as we used to at the Saturday movies. I carry it with me now whenever I give readings. Consider how like an ecstatic poem it is, this ball. Resilient. Agent of spontaneous friendship with strangers. Adored of dogs, lovingly chewed up, it kisses the ground and springs away to fall and kiss again and rest in any human hand its round and subtle energy.

A dream of south India comes. I tell Judith, who has an intuition. I add to it, then find a black rubber ball on my late afternoon path. I fool around in a lecture. Mary Oliver comes up to say she was walking her dogs and left that for me. I motion you away some now, dear reader, so we can get more arc on our poised exchange, this note.

Bridge

A forgotten memory came to me while I was reading a Seamus
    Heaney poem back across the Atlantic
        on the phone to Chloe, a poem about when Thomas

Hardy as a boy got down on all fours among sheep and looked
    in their bland faces and tried to
        feel how it was to be one. I was in the tub

as a boy when I heard my little sister coming and pretended
    to be drowned, curled under
        the bathwater, just an ear out to hear her intake

of breath and running to the living room where our parents
    were playing bridge with the
        Penningtons. A violent sliding back of chairs,

adult feet pounding. I go back under to my drowned self:
    am translated dripping, giving
        my naked foolery smile, like a dog lifted up

to wave bye-bye. The bridge players spank and hug me
    both. The hand must be redealt,
        bids forgotten. Mr. Penny howling, *It's a*

miracle, gollee, he rose from the dead! O slow of heart,
    take down this to read
        when I do actually die, no fooling.

A Swan. We Turn the Car Around to Look

Martha's Vineyard in January, island
    with seven, eight, or nine towns arranged
        around it: Tisbury, West Tisbury, Chilmark,
            Edgartown, Vineyard Haven, Menesha, and Oak

Bluffs, where we see a swan on the frozen
    lake, not stuck in it like the duck we heard
        about earlier today being pecked at by crows, with
            no way to dodge; it could only duck

with its neck, duck the crow. This swan alone on
    ice can walk and does, then sits on
        its big feet, soon, such dignity. No one we
            ask knows if it will stay through

winter, or if it's a day behind the flock,
    or a month, oblivious to cold, settled out
        on the open nowhere next a grey-silvering un-
            frozen center of pondwater. I love

when you say I love being in love with you, and I you,
    with dark lowering on this odd
        delicious sight, singular, the three of us,
            and the glide into liquid.

Luke and the Duct Tape

Nothing can save us. This sweetness dies and rots. Luke
    was a thirty-year-old
        pharmacy graduate student who worked at Horton-Add

Drugs, at the post office in the back that stays open
    until seven p.m., my p.o.
        It also has a lunch counter. He sometimes did

things behind there, like make me a tuna fish sandwich and
    fill a glass with ice and diet
        coke. He mopped the place and swept up, as quick

and accurate with the broom-jabs as he was at calculating my
    strange Tasmanian mail. *Hey,*
        Finland! Once when I sent out seventy-four books

priority mail, he said, *It looked like Christmas back*
    there. In the storeroom where the
        mailman picks up. He laughed so easily with his

quiet industry, something out of Normal Rockwell. He's
    maybe the most promising
        thing we are, Luke, young American man just before

he meets a woman and raises a family and does church group
    and little league, and every good
        thing stored in his strong hands comes building out

into the air. Luke, master of small fixing. Now on the
    glass double door, this
        handwritten posterboard for his memorial service,

11 a.m. today. I missed it. Would I have gone? Luke
    Poucher. I never knew a last
        name. One day we had some talk about how he knew

my name from all the mail, but I didn't know his. *Luke.*
    "That's a great name." He
        was killed instantly last Thursday in an automobile

accident down the street on Lumpkin at Old Princeton Rd.,
    where he lived, not half
        a mile from me, not a week ago. I hadn't heard and

don't now ask the Horton family for details. Car wreck,
    Luke's dead. Luke 17:12,
        The kingdom of God is within you. He was so

lightheartedly that, it took your breath. Is it with his
    death I fear my own before
        the loving here gets as open as it might could get

in such as me. I feel myself becoming arrogant sometimes
    and a little numb,
        insensitive, with this famousness I've been

absorbing the last few years. I do not understand Dylan
    Thomas' "Refusal to Mourn
        the Death of a Child By Fire in London." "After

the first death, there is no other," he concludes, but on
    what authority? He pictures
        his own death as entering "again the round Zion of

the water bead, . . . the synagogue of the ear of corn," and I
    have loved those words since
        I first heard them in 1957. I see the holy, tiny,

elemental corridors of corn grains and the fragile tearshape
    inside the word *Zion.* He says
        the nameless girl who burned to death is now

with the robed dead by the unmourning Thames water. It may
    be Luke is off somewhere
        profound and myriad, though I feel him close and

still-mortal as I write this, waiting for the foolish
    satisfaction of my own
        phrasing. What is the sudden subtraction of a

young man, who might just as well be my son, a filament of
    ocean beauty I do and don't
        see today, do. I grieve the death of Luke Poucher

for the place he swept and tended so well, this fivepointed
    threshing floor of stores
        and walkers and apartments, mailmen, depositors,

lunching retiree, chemo-waver, bodyworker, skateboarder, UPS,
    any bunch that knows each
        others' half-grin in hurried irritation out doing

errands. Let this be Luke, this end of the parking lot
    around the mailboxes, Luke
        Poucher Place. The air, the few flowers, and the

people as they meet going in to buy lunch or stamps or
    shampoo, their small nods
        of helplessness. I asked for duct tape once. *You*

know, we ought to carry that, but we don't. It's about all I
    know how to do to fix
        something. I've got some broken ducks. I need

to get them in a row. Let this low talking, the love and
    joking we do fumbling for
        courtesy here at the door be Luke, Luke looking up

from the stroke of his all-hallowing broom, *Beautiful*
    out there, idn't it?

Spring Morning

It's a spring morning in the 1940's when Ozella
    and my mother misunderstand each
        other. The exterminator man in his green

Orkin uniform coming up the walk, mother calls
    from the porch back to the kitchen.
        Do we have any bugs?

No'm, we used all those we had yesterday. She'd
    thought mother'd said bulbs, light
        bulbs, mother so elongated

her buuuuuuhhhhs, and barely put final consonants on
    at all. Now here's the bug man with
        his metal spray gun lying

down on the brick walk to laugh. We are so ready
    to laugh in the 1940's, we get down
        on our sides to enjoy it.

Whittling

John Templeton's great uncle Griff Verner
    spent much of his last days whittling neck-yokes
        for his chickens to wear so

they couldn't get through the wide slat divisions of
    his yard fence. There are other possible
        solutions to this problem, but eggs have

yolks, and Griff Verner's chickens had yokes, and he
    himself had that joke-job in a bemused
        neighborhood that watched every move. Somewhere

there's a crate of Griff's chicken yokes, I hope, as there's
    a wild shoebox of vision-songs
        stashed by a poet whose name we don't know yet,

nor the beauty and depth of his soulmaking, hers. Griff's
    white pine, Rembrantian fowl-collars may
        have also served as handles to wring their necks

with when Sunday demanded. John's grandmother's Methodist
    house had only two books in it, the *Holy
        Bible* and Fox's *Book of Martyrs.* When it rained,

there wasn't much to do indoors, and on Sundays nothing, no
    games, no deck of cards, no dominoes. Of course no
        television. I grew up in a house with no

TV in the 1940's and on into the mid-50's. We were in
    education. Sometimes at night there would be
        five different people in four different

rooms reading five different books. John says once his
    mother caught Sam and him playing cards
        on the floor. She snatched up the deck and said,

"Well, you can play cards in jail." There's always chores
    to do in the methodical world, no spare time to
        kill. Throw those idle gypsy two-faces in the trash.

Let them find other haphazard palms to occupy. John's
    father could carry on a side conversation
        with him while typing a sermon. John remembers

how as a child he would sit and talk with his dad and watch
    him do those two word things simul-manu-
        larynxactly together in the after-dinner Friday

night office. Griff Verner's whittling comes when you're
    not spry enough to chase chickens
        but still take some interest in the public's

consternation with oddness.

The Bay

An old man sitting on a bench poses this hypothetical
    to passers-by: if you found
        a paper sack full of money on the ground, tens

of thousands, what would you do? If I knew whose it was,
    I'd return it. Even if you
        found it at night? Yes, the next day I'd take it

back. You're a fool. He waves him on. Another citizen,
    same question. If money chanced
        to me that way, I'd keep it. Even if you knew

who lost it? Yes. You're a dangerous man, he says, looking
    away. Third guy. This story is not
        the same if a woman asks the question to three

women, is it? We'll come back to that. This one, How am
    I to know what dark mood, or lofty
        moral whim, or numbness, or light enthusiasm, or

urgent necessity, will surround me as part of what I do in
    the moment when I find the money?
        I do not know that, so I cannot answer. Sit down,

my friend. How have you been? Is it that any course decided
    on beforehand, any unspontaneous
        gesture, bears watching? We are blown about

a gusty bright afternoon; the wind comes veering, bumping
    us together, then away across
        the bay, affrighting, delighting, hilarious,

precarious, delerious, imperious, until we sink, that is
    die, because there is no shore
        to this: the waves in the woodgrain of the deck

flex their layer-lines against my fingerprint. It is a
    late afternoon, late April
        breeze I am looking up into as a cotton tree

releases its cotton like Normandy over the yard, the cars,
    the twelve concrete piers of a
        water tower that isn't here anymore. The tin

shed of an old bakery. As I watch and think to put such
    a natural floating in a poem,
        one of the sex-parachutes, a brave bewinded

sperm-jumper, lands just here, between my eyes.

Hillsize Cat

Our continuing research into what mind is, soul, love
    and deep being, spirit, memory,
        and the inner sun that makes everything radiant,

has brought this: the other night before sleeping I saw
    behind my closed eyes—what
        retina records those images—a huge, hillsize

cat stretched across, or sliding over, the curves of a
    river, another and another, the
        same cat with different riverscapes. Now reading

Raymond Carver's collected poems, *All of Us,* p.31, "As my
    body flies over water, as my soul,
        poised like a cat, hovers—then leaps into sleep."

Not a precise connection, but close enough to let me feel
    the brush of what gives art and
        dream, not to mention moments. Sleep and curl

inside a compassionate, image-generating, interpenetrative,
    electro-magnetic field of green
        riverwater catfur and rounded mountain. We are

talking this phenomenon in a line of connected porches
    curving along a gentle slant.
        Students are seated waiting for a teacher to start

the lecture. He's paging through his book. As I walk
    through, he nods to me, then begins.

Light on Leaves

With the light in the tree above Jittery Joe's, I am
      wondering about energy
            exchange: the sun gives itself wholly to the

tree and us all, but the leaves on this side get
      additional nightime attention
            from artificial light, whose power derives from

water falling sixty feet off a dam to turn a turbine.
      I don't know how any of this
            works, least of all chlorophyll, what out of

sunlight and earthen minerals and magical moisture makes
      oak leaves by the bushel basket.
            Some exchange not unlike this must go on between

people: the enlightened ones and the near-to and the goofy
      joyful ones and those that dance
            their ignorance with those that laugh melodious

and others who play like roots in the dirt. The various
      flavors of lightedness take human
            form and compose their waking motions to enjoy the

music of conversation. This is a pecan, its double trunk
      growing through a seam in the
            cement. And of course it's like us in the nearly

constant noise of fivepointed traffic, how we live so fierce
      and shamed and free, too busy,
            and lovingly bentover with our nut-bearing gift.

The Ant

With normal ignorance, I follow this elegant ant crossing
　　my page before I can think of
　　　　a thing. The ballpoint falls in behind like

buddies across the desert. They angle up and left, northwest,
　　northeast off the paper, back on
　　　　and down southeast, making a fair freehand

coastline of the north end of the Persian Gulf. I began
　　the line well down the western
　　　　shore from Kuwait. This was moments before or as

the Dhahran bombing at the American compound, killing nineteen.
　　About then, I was tracking my ant,
　　　　wondering *what's right there*. He knew I was

dogging him, but stayed unalarmed, didn't quicken his pace, had
　　a map to sketch. A Mercedes fuel
　　　　truck with a Swiss mechanism stops at the gate; it

and the getaway go left to the empty lot. There is a drawing
　　my mother made one Tuesday afternoon
　　　　in 1970 in a letter I still have. She had seen

my office in the English Department, exclaimed at the red oak
　　window-companion, holder of nest,
　　　　moulder of acorn. "When the leaves come off, draw

me that tree." She does a few limbs on a central trunk. "Looks
　　like my chest x-ray," she jokes.
　　　　The oak died and was cut down by the grounds crew.

Mother's winter diagnosis was lung cancer, dead by May. The
　　great mulberry flourishes in place
　　　　of the oak in my office vista. Seven crows land

on the fruiting crown and begin idle harvest, urged to change
　　perch periodically by young
　　　　squirrels. Very lively scene here out my unopenable

glass. The bomb: forty-eight living rooms harpooned with shards of
    picture window. Those who
        had gone to bed now sleep with their shoes on. Others,

the night owls, died and are buried. My son is remodeling my
    kitchen. The old sink upsidedown
        in the backyard prior to being hauled to the dump,

its scummy drainage nub in the air, makes a perfect roost for
    the owl I've been glimpsing
        from down the driveway. Wideawake in the daytime,

here's another high-spirited omen of death. Who can praise
    quickly enough the truth
        of how we are here on a walk or a trip to the mall

to buy a toy refrigerator and two or three shirts, or how with
    due panache we appear on
        television, then each alone in too much traffic?

I say we can praise quickly, if not enough. The ant walks
    into my sleeping ear, and it's
        inside the sun where we sit and laugh like Shadrach,

Meshach, and Abednego, a furnace honeycomb of hallways made
    of gold and grapeskin-glaucous light.

Talking the Night with a Gentleman in Green

Khe San, where the human wave assault comes before dawn, their walking wounded first, drugged up enough to die on top of the concertina wire. The next wave used those dying bodies to jump to the next, mostly picked off before they got to our trenches. Then the third wave with real soldiers, pure hell every day.

Waiting through the night was worst, them yelling *Hey American, you die.* His, a sniper company, working in pairs or threes. They talk on the phone some still, about going to see the wall, the night they got in a barfight.

One time he was with a group of eight playing cards under a tree, gin rummy, no poker chips. A tank round hit the tree and seven of the eight, all but him, died instantly. I have no idea what *died instantly* means. I was taking my American Poetry Since World War II class out to protest the war, daring to do so, born in 1937, too old for Vietnam, too young for Korea, no war for me.

War is academic. I had my finger dislocated once and pulled straight and my ankle bent back and permanently weakened in football practice when Ellis Goodloe flattened me like statuary holding an extra point. Surely that's illegal now, to run through the holder.

Kenny ran out to haul in a buddy. Machine guns cut him off at the shins. He felt nothing, kept stubbing away, then crawling with his friend on his back, North Vietnamese knives all over and around being shot off by other Americans in the trenches. He got back, but the one he went for was dead.

He's not that close to the two that survived from his company, three of forty-three. They'd like to get in another barfight. I'm not into that anymore. I just like to hear what people are passionate about. What do you love? Like you and this Rumi. I like that.

There was a Mexican-American guy who'd come down the line every night and talk to us and make us feel great. There was some deep joy in his smile, in the midst of all that shit. Every night he'd walk along talking to everybody individually. We caught a short round, a mortor from our side, and it took him out.

Nobody said anything, but we went and stood by his body and got inside his smile again, one at a time. It was a line of seven hundred men, nobody saying anything. I didn't know that Mexican-American's name, but he was beyond the ordinary. Then this chaplain comes in a helicopter and tries to comfort and counsel us. When he flew off, a round hit the chopper and blew the crew and chaplain to pieces, damndest thing.

Kenny can walk well without his feet and lower legs, until the infection there in the nubs chafing against the prosthesis comes back. When it does, he uses crutches, or wheelchair. Beauty is to see what people love. I paid my taxes and let the war go on and on, as sometimes I let the television stay talking to itself when I go out on an errand.

We sent Kenny on an errand and filmed it for documentary footage. My family had a set of antique ivory dominoes that felt so neat to the hand. I would line them up and they'd lean softly across each other like Asia going communist with the sound of silk slippers on an ivory staircase. Kenny's soul is durable and definite like the Ford tractor I learned how to drive on.

He has questions. What is addiction? Why do some people make us flow like fire? Some people go to a war, but they're not really there in it. I haven't visited the wall. I do not know if I have the courage to risk being shot to bits for next to nothing, when a friend is out where nobody lives.

I had a friend named Gamble Rogers, who was walking on a Florida beach at dark. He was from the north Georgia mountains, couldn't swim a lick. Alone, he heard a young boy floundering in the surf. Gamble rushed in the water, and they both drowned. Sometimes you have to do it, if you're there.

Many of us newshounds do not hate ourselves enough in our studies considering Kosovo. I feel disaster building. Security breaks down. Four hundred thousand dead of anthrax in Kansas City. Fresno unlocatable. We don't hate how it's been enough, or we don't love enough: these pedestrian fatalities, Mary and Martha, fourth grader twins, getting off the bus at their babysitter's.

I heard the brakes and saw the smoke says *grandma*, what the neighborhood children call her, seventy-seven. She's looked after nearly all of them on Yellow Creek Drive. It was a white pickup pulling an orange tractor driven by Raphael Escobar. The flashing STOP on the school bus was extended, which we're all supposed to know means traffic *bothways* stops at plenty of distance. Raphael is a recent immigrant and didn't know. He pulls around to pass. The children are running because they're *free*. It's *afterschool*.

I sit on the top step with a woman calling 911, groaning. A line of twelve hundred refugees walks parallel the railroad track in Kosovo. A Serbian policeman takes a young girl out of line and throws her in front of the train. Train passes. The father jumps down and tries to put the girl's head back on the body. We need film to show, close in, the policeman's face, the girl's, then slow along the line of refugees, father, brother, how each face keeps and loses light.

I hold this truth to be self-evident. That all men are capable of sustained murderous rage that can go on for months, that can reoccur years afterward, submerge and go cold and secret and do tremendous damage and not care. That we best not give that father a loaded assault rifle or a truckload of explosives or any weapon of mass destruction.

Whenas in the course of human events, young boys attack the courtyard area between shop and English or the library and the lunchroom trying to kill those who have tormented them, or perhaps they haven't, the men who are fathers and uncles and the men who are friends of those men had better spend more time with those boys, telling them stories and wrestling with them and throwing around whatever ball it is the season of, showing them how to use two hands and cradle it next time, whenas.

To honor the mystery of a single human life, we could try not to use the weaponry we've spent so much to devise. The Canberra Commission on the Elimination of Nuclear Weapons says three things they think are true: 1. If nuclear weapons exist, they will be used. 2. Any use is a catastrophe. 3. When people understand this, the majority say *No*, they don't want that to happen. Inevitability, catastrophic effect, and democratic rule. We must not override the will and compassion of the people.

Years ago I dialed a wrong number; a woman answered. She was evidently waiting for terrible news or had just gotten the world's worst. In such stunned grief she couldn't explain I had the wrong number. Oh no no oh oh no no nooh no no She hung up. I hung up.

Abscission Leaf, Looking into Water

A night-sleeping rain, become now these
    puddle-windows where we watch
        the others' eyes in a wet field:

how we are *not* dead and buried!
    The bread-push underfoot: loved ones
        in a spherical bed so wide and round we

stretch your left sole to my right to
    (wicker worsa) walk as each the other's path:
        waking and dream in a kiss-touch

continuum: breath-faces moving at the mirror-lip
    bahbah bahbahbah, as when I did observe
        under the glass skin: turtle moving moss

thread, a frog's one-eye wink, before school or any
    fear of the talking-knot tightening
        in my stuck throat, rather its opposite

release, what scientists call the abscission layer
    circling the stem where it lets go and
        begins fly-fall: the gingko

has an abscission leaf which when it goes, the rest
    will not be long: her yellow
        slip slips as we turn to see

and feel the abscission words loosen: night
    ensuing night, their resinous balsam,
        carry my slow-spilled dose,

and a long river-silence flows in the juice: a red
    blackspotted tupelo leaf and a
        yellow fivepointed sweetgum rise off

the silt floor turning their tips to touch
    the surface from the other side
        and sail: I am lying asleep in a

nightriver room strobed with boatlight sidling
the curve, its engine throb below
the cliff boiling the churn and mix.

Silo, Spring Violets

By the violets in the watercress
    new grass under the slender ash
        trees by the rooted-river spidery

bankedge, I fold in with edible lavender
    butterflies, each next each in
        a wandering myth of body, and

crows. I do not know who I am,
    or ever will, who invite friends
        to see a silo of memory

whose house is an empty plot between
    an uncovered well and this other
        cylinder of poured concrete. We

go clumped together as a kind of a way
    for a while, then take our single stems
        aloof. Listening to music

in the dark, I feel a great sphere of violets
    and water and grass riding in the night between
        us and the moon. It cannot be

looked at directly; it's more elusive than even
    our fluttering stories that leave a
        silky damp in the air.

The Final Final

I missed giving my final final exam. I slept through it. The alarm didn't sound, or I turned it off in my sleep. I'm buying a new clock. But maybe it's perfect this way. They wrote me such letters. I'll give them all A's. But that moment will not come back, no matter how I call, howl for it to, weep. This morning will not come back this afternoon.

But the letters I have from them are better than the finals they might have written, maybe not. This class really was the best I ever, and I regret. I regret, though this way may really be truly right, it hurts so missing the saying goodbye to each as they come up, my best, my last. I did that last lecture class well enough, a week ago Thursday. That was good, I guess. And they wouldn't have written what they did if I had been there today.

Unconsciously, I gave them my absence, as these last eleven years my teacher has consciously given me his absence-presence, whatever however he is with me now he's dead. Problem is, is. While we're in these aging shapes to show up for class, bright eyes, bright ears. Seems like so much else in my life, the waking late and not making the formal gathering, and this regret for sleeping through.

I cannot believe I missed the final final. The predictable conclusion to my legend in the English Department. The secretaries loved it. I can't believe it, and I won't say I'm sorry. I *am* sorry, like my mother used to call unreliable hired help. You can't count on him; he's just sorry. You never know if he'll show up. I'm so sorry I won't say I'm sorry.

And actually it gives me a chance to give 40 A's, which out of some arrogant ungenerous grading attitude I would not have done, which now I do, with an iron whang of the Grades Only chute door in the back of the Academic Building, and an illegal pull of the chapel bell.

Do you reckon I'll sleep through my death, another pull, sleep through Resurrection Day, another, and have to do this whole jabbering career again, pull, or will I get to go on to some other plane where there's no such thing as dreamless sleep and discipline and drinking too much the night before and faulty clocks and forgetfulness and the frustration of saying anything in front of groups, and no such a thing as regret and the satisfaction of a job well done, and no more ceremonial walk-through doors, and no way to miss the living moments, and no way to try to write them right.

Or say there's nothing after now. Then that lovely bunch of young people talking and laughing and writing me letters, forgiving me even, straggling out of that room made sacred by our presences and attention, were gone when I arrived at 10:45. You created quite a stir around here says someone on the hall bench. I bet. I heard them say you've used up your poetic license.

This is how death might surprise, as the thing undone, irremediably missed-out-on. You round a corner and the backyard party with your friends is breaking up. Where have you been! Alone, asleep. If I lived with someone, I might have been jogged awake, reminded, but I still don't want to live with anyone.

I'm unrepentently, sufficiently, some would say terribly, alone. Look at me and be frightened of not pouring the last of the love and wakefulness you're given, which is every moment, but moreso some than others. Emptying out is the point. In time, over time, be early.

Currycombing

This woman currycombs her brown stallion, Dervish,
    in an open stableyard.
        She pats and coos and rubs and traces

muscle-thread from haunch to knee, shoulder to hip,
    radiating each thew, ear-rim,
        lash, moaning into the huge raked and roiling

body, as if she were the invisible being who supposedly
    tends this world. Supposedly
        nothing. She picks his sheath clean of flakes of

rotted black skin, combs and flickers there, a common
    practice. He is her doorway,
        where what is touched flames and consciously

mirrors back, a conversation of leg and groin to along and
    down, breezy lovers before
        and after in sweetness not of consummation, but

the whooing exchange the dervishes call *sohbet,* one step
    above meditation, which
        is a step up from prayer. She swirls the triple

spiral of Newgrange, the map of midsummer snaking in
    to wake our burial mound
        forehead of stone. This woman makes that

again and again on the side of her horse. So slip your hand
    into whatever you use
        for a currycomb. Feel the layered pack alive

beneath words—field, faces, hue, tone, chip, grain—the
    twitch of overlapping melody
        as you and your animal are talking.

Pans of Color

Dream students, numb-dumb, half-dead. I try to wake
    them by putting pans of
        paint on the floor, reds, yellows, rust, and

buttery orange. They sit in the pans, then on the floor,
    imprinting their undersides'
        leafshapes, flopping like rabbits around the room

making an overlapping autumn ground, cones of how we press
    against the earth, each
        underthigh loinrump a master brush, its wrist and

fingers this October afternoon befringeing. The first thing
    I tried to find words for was
        fall color: twelve years old. I still despair.

ald Hall
Don   Is Fall
ing Down

(LONDON BRIDGE)

Donald Hall *is* falling, and I can't catch him. Not
   seeing the little stepdown
      at the bottom of the slanted chapel aisle, he

falls in slowmotion, to his knees, then sidewise to
   shoulder. His dear head does
      not hit. *I'm OK.* There's a long getting up,

three-quarters of the audience there. He raises one hand
   in mock triumph. This is
      the first poetry reading of his eighth decade,

magnificent, tender, broken open with naked grief.
   Afterward, after the signing
      and the jokes and the serious student advice,

he and I sit beaming our eyes at each other, side by side
   at the Holiday Inn bar. What
      I most loved about the night was that from the

fall to now, I took his arm with both my hands wherever
   we went, out the chapel, down the
      steps, along the walk, across the street, around

the corner to the Globe, up the stairs, down the stairs. I
   walked him like an older
      brother who'd had a stroke, and he let me. We

talked so sweetly shuffling along. He 70, me 61. He's
   absolutely fine without
      anyone holding to him, but it was so precious that

muttering and tottering around the September Athens night.
    I recommend it. Fall flat
        before the altar of poemgiving and see if a

friend isn't tenderized into some fresh foolishness the
    two of you will never outlive.

Hyssop

I'm sitting alone at the forlorn concrete table outside KFC eating my three-piece chicken-only original-recipee when a black man parks and gets out and comes over. He moans, That poooor Bill Clinton. What do you mean? They set him up, lookahere. They knew he was married when they went to his room. And Hillary. I heard she jumped on his bandwagon when it got started down in Arkansas. See?

White House people say there's not much love between them. It's an arrangement. Tripp had a book deal cooking way back. They all got something to sell. Bill Clinton is a lonely man. This is his birthday. That dress, why was she keeping that dress and not having it cleaned? They set him up good. He's just trying to get a little comfort.

Lookaherenow. If he was to get on international tv and get down on his knees like King David. Clean me with hyssop, Lord. *Lookaherenow hyssop.* Think what that would do. He got a chance to change some lives. Both arms extended up, he goes into the Kentucky Fried and comes immediately back out. I just got one thing. He got a big chance.

In this current ugly, meanspirited time, I would like to invoke a new rule for whoever wants to talk about Bill Clinton's sexual life, the Jesus John 8 rule is to be enforced publically in the media, on the talk shows, and privately with two friends standing in line at a coffee house.

Jesus comes to temple early. He has been sitting with a group all morning. They're not in the sanctuary proper but in "the treasury," which must be some kind of courtyard with a dirt floor. Some pharisees arrive, the traditional literalists who are so threatened by Jesus' message of forgiveness and unconditional love and by the instant, intimate availability of God to each individual without an intermediary priesthood. Jesus is putting them out of business; they're trying to catch him in some inconsistency with the Old Testament.

This time they bring a woman caught in the act of adultery. There are some tremendously inhuman passages in *Deuteronomy* about punishing sexual conduct. *Deut. 22:23-24: If a damsel that is a virgin be betrothed unto an husband, and a man find her in the city and lie with her, then ye shall bring them both out unto the gate of that city and ye shall stone them with stones until they die.*

This is the judgmental cruelty Jesus is trying to change. I love how he does it. *Jesus stooped down and with his finger wrote on the ground as though he heard them not.* They insist he make a judgment. Jesus looks up. Everyone knows what he says next. *He that is without sin among you, let him cast the first stone.* He bends back and resumes writing in the dirt, or maybe just making a design, waiting and doodling, letting the gentleness of his presence settle in.

One by one the pharisees leave *beginning at the eldest, even unto the last.* Every bozo gone, Jesus talks to her. *Where are your accusers? Hath no man condemned thee?* No man, Lord. *Neither do I condemn thee: go and sin no more.* I like to think she stays and listens to the next part, where Jesus himself is almost stoned to death. He talks with amazing daring about who he is, his lineage and how it supercedes the Jewish line through Abraham. *Before Abraham was, I am.* (John 8:58) Outside of time, this is the mystery itself talking.

Some who hear him pick up stones, but they don't throw them. It's not time. This is the rule: if you want to talk about Clinton's sex life, or anybody's, first tell a recent sexual secret of your own. Throw in a lot of detail; be willing to be grilled with any amount of ancillary questions. You masturbated in the shower yesterday afternoon? Who did you think of? Who have you fantasized about previously?

You must tell the full truth sparing no detail, naming all names, volunteering further information. This goes on for as long as anyone present can stand it. Who's first? Sam Donaldson? Cokie? Rather, you rascal. Wolf. Leslie! King David's contrition about his lust for Bathshaba is heard in Psalm 53. *Purge me with hyssop, and I shall be clean.* Hyssop is an aromatic, bitter herb with spikes and delicate small blue flowers. Bundles of hyssop twigs represent the stinging, tender learning our desires lead us through, the low scrub.

Seagull at the Newark Airport

Going low less than a foot off the asphalt, then up over
    a tanker truck and around
        the freestanding staircase, a poem with its

two black beads watches how government manages to fly.

The Mill

When I was teaching, this was the exhausted time, mid-May,
        having gone on every day on
                the quarter system. They still come up and hug

me, but after another year, no young person around here will
        remember how I read the
                E. A. Robinson poem and stopped at the starry velvet

image to ask, What *could* he have been thinking?

Animal

This is an animal you must imagine: part fox, part weasel,
    part burrowing owl and
        dwarf. You are this animal, digging the tunnel

of your secret. You scratch and scratch, and you have found
    the ore. The vein is
        infinitely mineable, inside the trance of work.

Now there's a soft-winged coo outside above you. Your hands
    stop pawing to listen: doves.

Observing English 102 the Day
They Do "The Red Wheelbarrow"

A late afternoon class with a few older students. I'm
    thinking, because I'm not
        doing the teaching, somebody forgot to get

his tools in, because if you leave a wheelbarrow out
    glazing in the rain for
        long, it'll not be one anybody can depend on.

I've done it twice, had a handle break when it was
    loaded with stone. So we
        lie sometimes when we talk about poems and

let a pastoral wish, or what we've never
    lifted, be a good
        enough way to spend the afternoon.

Emily Song

Of all sounds made by water, by ground and its
    inhabitants, she heard
        the the most natural note from a cricket.

    But witness for her land,
    And witness for her sea,

    The cricket is the utmost
    Of elegy to me.

          (1775, J)

The whirr of being embodied lives in her ear, a watch
    going off: *eeeeee,*
        durrrr, durrrruuuurrt

Several years ago, a dream of Joe Campbell. He and I
    sitting on my mother's
        bed in the old house. I am telling him how I

love to sing Emily Dickinson to old Appalachian hymn
    parts. *We do that*
        all the time in heaven, he says. Different

tune each try, I've no notion what will come out
    my cricket mouth.

    Exultation is the going
    Of an inland soul to sea,
    Past the houses
    Past the headlands,
    Into deep eternity

    Bred as we among the mountains,
    Can the sailor understand

The divine intoxication
Of the first league out from land?

(143. F)

Now she stands, as all we must, weirdly vertical
    beside a corpse.

O give it motion, deck it sweet
With artery and vein
Upon its fastened lips lay words
Affiance it again
To that pink stranger we call dust
Acquainted more with that
Than with this horizontal one
That will not lift its hat

(1550. F)

Affiance, fierce and desolate, obsolete verb meaning
        put it back together, make
            another pink stranger, fiancée me, marry

dust with lightstruck juice again. What is the spurt
        that lifts our hat, the
            nod coming through our *isolato* chorale?

The blackberry wears a thorn in his side
But no man heard him cry.

We tell a hurt to cool it
This mourner to the sky
A little further reaches instead
Brave blackberry.

(548, F)

Jesus is a June-Georgia blackberry, sweet-tart, I reach
    through briary prickle to
        pick, whose blood transubstantiaties to mine.

And the image of Buddha slumps like a mound of mashed
    potatoes smiling at two
        people smoothing their growly sexual brains out.

Emily has this love that wants the spry arms of the wind
    to carry her somewhere to
        touch her wick to whose? It doesn't and it

does matter her candle has gone out.

    My process is not long
    The wind could wait without the gate
    Or stroll the town among.

    To ascertain the house
    And is the soul at home
    And hold the wick of mine to it
    To light, and then return

        (802, F)

And don't we all want to come back here? Where
    she stands in her nightgown,
        fire-colored stranger calling ocean water,

    An everywhere of silver

        (931, F)

    To my quick ear the leaves conferred
    The bushes they were bells
    I could not find a privacy
    From nature's sentinels

In cave if I presumed to hide
The walls begun to tell
Creation seemed a mighty crack
To make me visible

(912, F)

Yet she hid like no other, who could find no privacy
     from music and waking and
          this continuous revelation of how it goes:

Finding is the first act
The second, loss,
Third, expedition for the golden fleece

Fourth, no discovery
Fifth, no crew
Finally, no golden fleece
Jason, sham, too

(910, F)

Tall latté at 5:30, a passionate mind across to talk
     what evidence we have of
          the animal side of the beloved, O courteous,

magnificent and common presence we swim, weather we
     walk, self we share,
          wild true beeswax addressed with every poem.

One and one are one
Two be finished using
Well enough for school
But for minor choosing

(497, F)

Emily's new math, lookahere, one and one are one. So
    how is it when the heart
        opens? Some feel it as a poet says the music

of herself, or his. Some feel it in the presence of dogs,
    or horses. Some as a day
        of construction work cranks up, the bunch in

the office-loading dock area joking and wondering. Some
    on late afternoon walks with
        a granddaughter; some when the movie lights dim

in anticipation. How often did she go to the store? Did
    any man ever undress her,
        button by hook? Some as they sit in patient

scribblery, pen-out-page-open to the Damascus marketplace
    labyrinth of language.
        Some with the sudden death of a friend.

    My garden like the beach
    Denotes there be a sea
    That's summer
    Such as these the pearls
    She fetches such as me

        (469, F)

The pearls are vegetables from her garden, flowers, shells
    off the beach, poems,
        letters, friends, whatever grows or gets given by

beach and garden and mailman, or stranger walking up. Here's
    another doodly tangent,
        another chipmunk flower, another moody dogpath

snaking another Emily chant to raise the dead. I see her as
    a child in church. I hear
        Etheridge doing Willow weep for me, in a prison cell,

Willow weep for me..., my mother going Casey would waltz with
the strawberry blonde, and the
band played on. He'd whirl round the floor with

the girl he adored, and the band played on.... This world is
a house where anyone at
any time may spring through to song, yes it is.

And Emily may well be horrified at my belting out her beribboned
fascicles, starting them from
hiding. Excuse me dear. These are too rambunctious

to stay in storage. Did you forget them each as you put them
away? Did you look back?
Had you time some Wednesday afternoon? Did your genius

visit in the morning? Did you get up in the middle of the night
to commune with that
mysterious one? In a parking lot in San Francisco,

winter 1984, you are a man this time in a cardboard box reading
outloud a waterspout exuberance
and volcanic sorrow. I join you. When you finish,

we will go out to those brick steps for a smoke. And look at
some sky that's open to being
song, clouds eliding with the land dew-wet and blue.

Joel

Yesterday I met a man in his eighties. I called
    him *Bud,* and he
        hugged me. He likes to paint watercolors of

bark. Closeup loving texture: oak bark at sunset,
    black tupelo in early
        afternoon. He sometimes sings phrases

of Hebrew. I wonder why I'm here in these hallways
    today, sight corridors,
        anywhere. *The Song of Songs*: a davening

nod goodbye, damp-smeared color. Nothing hurting
    at the moment, backpain
        gone. Death is a curved heavy slab of bark.

You feel it pushing away from you, a door inward. I
    will send Joel some
        bark, a gourd, a note, and this poem

which would like to become a psalm.

Chapel Green

I wake laughing: we were sitting thinking up new
    books for the Bible:
        between Peter and Paul a small New Testament

classic called *Cheeses*. Another, *An Account of the Road*
    Between Here and Hebron.
        For the Old Testament, *Sacajawea: The Hebrew*

Years and *Dingaling: Three Months in an Ice Cream*
    Truck. There need to
        be additions to the old anthology. Say the

Gospel of Thomas, translated by Marvin Meyer, Afterword
    by Harold Bloom. The kingdom
        of God is inside you and all around you.

Saying #3. There's no narrative to this gospel; it's
    just what Jesus says. No
        crucifixion, no resurrection. Jesus performs

no miracles and dies for no one's sins. Saying #5: Know
    what is in front of your
        face, and what is hidden from you will be

disclosed. There's a lot about the *kingdom*. A woman is
    carrying a jar of meal.
        She doesn't know the handle is broken with meal

spilling out behind her. She reaches home and sets the jar
    down empty. Her seeing
        then is the *kingdom*: a state the sufis call

majesty. A man has treasure he doesn't know about
    buried in his field. He
        dies. The field goes to his son, who also fails

to discover what's there. The son sells the field to
    another man, who plows
        and happens to find the treasure. It's not that

son and father didn't plow. A pure depth of being, *the*
　　kingdom, is spread out on
　　　　the earth. I am light over all things. I am

all: from me has come forth and to me all has reached.
　　Split a piece of wood;
　　　　I am there. Lift up a stone; you will find me there.

When you make the two into one, and when you make the inner
　　like the outer and the outer
　　　　like the inner, and the upper like the lower,

and when you make the male and female into a single one, so
　　that the male will not be
　　　　male nor the female female, then you will enter

the kingdom. These words kept in a dry clay jar in a cave
　　in upper Egypt for two
　　　　thousand years, until December 1945, a cold overcast

day. Workers come on camels looking for *sabakh,* accumulations
　　of bird droppings they use
　　　　for fertilizer. One of them smashes the jar with his

mattock and sees "a gold substance fly out in the air and
　　disappear," papyrus feathers
　　　　from the Nag Hammadi library. The gold dust of Jesus'

sentences shoots into us as fertilizing pollen. In the chapel
　　I grew up playing inside
　　　　there was a wooden plaque on the back wall.

The kingdom of God is within you, Luke 17:12. The Thomas
　　collection says what we're
　　　　looking for has come and we do not know it.

All around and inside too, we're everywhere in the act of
　　finding it. Be passersby.
　　　　Show me the stone the builders rejected. That is the

cornerstone. The sealed jar was beside a huge boulder fallen
    in the talus below the cliff
        called Jabal al-Tarif. In the front of that chapel

is a window with the twelve-year-old Jesus amazing the elders.
    Their puzzled expressions, his
        sky-blue tunic with its border of red and gold

and white. The side windows were an amber that turned light
    green in spring. In graduate
        school I wrote a poem for my father's retirement

in which I imagine him missing terribly the field of leaves
    that poured in around his chapel
        talks. May again, and the gold spring sundown

air of that hill will fly out in ordinary sentences.

So Close, Not a Foot

Harrison and 7th, Leadville, Colorado, April 8, 2000,
    about 7 p.m., crossing
        from a coffeehouse to the Delaware Hotel,

rubberlegged and rubberarmed from driving into the new
    height, ten thousand two
        hundred feet above sea level, I step out

after two cars go by not seeing the third, small white
    blindspotted mobile. My
        love Judith says a faint, *don't go*. I hold

up. Faces in the car window upturn to me like an
    unfolding cotton tablecloth
        so close, not a foot. Where I could easily

have ceased to see out these coffee eyes: become a
    mangled, dragged-along, inroaded,
        gravel-clumped sog-sod bag of *don't go*.

And that topfloor sunset tall-window turn-of-the-century
    room would not have held
        our membraneous circulations so soon after.

My hand on your face's curve, I ask for useful fear and
    letting go whatever won't
        allow words to come; I am so glad to be here.

Love for Clouds

There was a time when a man said poems and friendship
    grew visible. Whole
        evenings, phrases came out of his mouth

like breasts. Language nourished with silence as an
    infant opening for the
        nipple: naked words appear and enter

the listeners. It is not strange and dreamlike. It
    feels natural and fully
        awake. *This* might seem strange, my standing

reading words on paper. I look up and speak and look
    down. But I do not apologize.
        Now is no less wonderful than then. We write

in a coffeehouse or parked alone in a car. We print
    pages and revise on the
        porch for months, years, tinkering. I am

climbing through a mist rising off the Tennessee river
    in the 1940's, down a bluff.
        No one knows I am. On the shale ledges

that slant and shelve into the water are stone seashells:
    fossils from the ocean
        that lived when fish spoke cloud shoals

in the bright milk-mind of this child.

1971 and 1942

What does Yeats mean, *The heart grows old?* The impulse
   toward romance and sexual need
      less sharp? I have a friend who's made

himself a saint of lust, MacIntyre! It is a quiet
   birdless sabbath night
      as I read Lowell, his final doubt of the

messiah. I admire his effort to say what guidance we
   get in this clarifying of
      unique light. Can we learn to listen? To what

and how and where? Just before dawn, one candle in the
   cabin. Can we follow what
      we're shown? Is disobedience also the way and

patience an unnecessary suffering? What does it mean to
   me, *The heart grows old.*
      A few memories of my mother, dead now thirty

years. Her belief, when pressed, was that the world
   began with Adam and Eve
      in 4004 B.C., a Monday morning, January 1st.

When I went off to college and graded papers in the Religion
   Department at the University of
      North Carolina, we had a running argument about

that oriental document, Genesis B, my mother and me, she
   on her couch-nest flustered,
      I arrogant and cool in dad's chair. Carbon

dating phased her less than my dating. Mother had the
   innate joy of morning's
      fresh matter, the shine of October in the South.

The war effort, the victory garden and victory goats and
   rams and cows running loose
      over the campus. The magical cattle guard

gate, a xylophone under the zephyr. I used to go pretend
grocery shopping on my tricycle.
Out from the cool moss walk no sun ever hit,

into the sun, pick up some leaves and rocks, make a circle
inside the tower and come
back with the goods. Umm, good. What is this?

Fried chicken. What is this? Butter pecan ice cream.
Every day was an adventure
for my mother, and scary. Afraid of cars, the

bluff, afraid of hurting and falling, mice and snakes and
roaches. She never drank.
She woke pure emanation. I give myself her

mornings again, and listen to be led. Last night I was
shown in dream how to be
in front of a group without notes, or maybe

my fear of that. Anyway, no more arrant new critical
chicanery. I bow to the
mother of morning and laughter, and to the father

of smoke. My father's heart did and did not grow old. He
was bored and bitter sometimes,
but the last six weeks of his life he was

more open than anyone I've seen, filled with a big no-worry, no
holding back love for everyone he
met. He could see their souls there valiantly

embodied, singing their solo peeps however they must. Mother
died in early May, he the 3rd
of July, bending to kiss the plume of a lobby

water fountain. There's an ache in me when I say 1971 and
1942, a hollow *holler!*
That's how the heart grows old, re-inhabiting

the five-year-old and thirty-four-year-old grown old,
    empty and fragile with
        working. It's the end of some summer. My parents

are sitting out on the bluff as the sun goes down, in
    those homemade adirondack chairs.
        Here comes the Lake Queen excursion boat

around the far bend under Lookout with its watery tingle of
    dance music and the second
        level which is all dance-floor, and when they

slide past this bluff, some of them will come to the railing
    and wave. I'll pull one
        of these heavy wooden chairs over and sit with them,

Hub and Bets. What else might I do with this evening? The
    reading and writing work
        must wait on this love. One thing we children

would do was yell across the river and Williams Island and the
    river again straight into Elder
        Mountain. Our voices came back small and perfected.

Just vowels were best, *ooooooooooooooooo*, but also short
    sentences like *I can't hear you,*
        or *Call me Raccoon,* which was its other name.

We played at letting the mountain say outloud our given names,
    while it was always saying
        with its deep green voice our most secret selves

to this day. I can't untangle the feeling of being exhausted
    with the beauty of wind in
        in the top of those trees and not here.

Now here. We slip through to another view, yet we haven't
    left. The heart grows
        keen, quicker, and less here.

None Other

We were leaning against the hood of my pewter
    Silverado and I told
        her how I came to buy it, which is not

the point here. I re-told a fairytale she had heard
    of but did not know, and
        she told me about a person she had taken

three months off to help heal. None of this is the
    reason I'm working pen
        and paper on the upstairs porch after midnight.

It's how when we hugged goodbye, my hand went innocently
    under her shirt to touch
        the warm silken back. The feel of a woman's

skin is my subject. Along with the bridge of dying, my
    granddaughter's skippy dance
        across, water, and this elegant need to write.

Fly

Say we actually are as alert as the black fly, wide as
    a quarter here in the woods,
        that I never see until I pour out much-clotted

sour milk beside the cabin deck, and seconds later they're
    thick in the clabber.
        Same as when today the pipes are broken

and I have to use the forest floor for facilities. Before
    I have my pants back up,
        they're on the stool. I know a piano player who

whirls himself around saying *I have perfect stool.* Are
    they everywhere, or do
        they come instantly from anywhere as we put out

the slimy hors d'oevres they adore: the motion of grace to
    a sharp-felt prayer: Kosovo
        this Easter, my son Benjamin's marriage

breaking. Black fly, rise and light on this rot we've made.
    Massage it with your myriad
        modified mouthparts back to mulch

and cool dark crumble through the fingers.

Bawa's Presence

In another dream my friend Jonathan shows me how Bawa's
    presence stays in him.
        He flexes his bicep and a bone-muscle tchuringa-like

flange springs up from the arm extending out the classroom
    window into sky. Part of
        my connection to Bawa is that I can fly-climb

and touch this aboriginal carrier of ancestral power
    generated from Jonathan's
        arm. In my hovering I realize that the currency of

Rumi's poetry is from Bawa and that I sometimes can show his
    presence in my eyes. I
        walk around shy in this continuing friendship,

feeling the tremendous grace of his blending with us. Finally
    as answer to Jonathan's
        impressive show, I flex my bicep and out flows

a spaghetti-like fountain of energy-slivers, demonstrating
    comically how each
        combination of personal with light is unique.

Winter

And ready for Khidr the green ancient, my interior
    tastily decorated with empty
        wine bottles, a stack of four inflated truck

innertubes with Christmas lights dangled down inside,
    two bags of Portland cement
        turned too hard anymore to use, two two-gallon

kerosene containers, a plastic bottle of bubble-making
    juice, and a package of
        hummingbird food waiting for March.

Stone

Comes a sequence after sixty: set them in the earth
    from the gate to the shed
        you're beginning to use more. Like the visit

to Southwest Guilford County High School in Greensboro,
    N.C.: a kid raises his hand
        seventeen rows back, "What're we doing here?"

It's 2:25 in the afternoon. I've explained three times
    we're writing a quick
        half-page about some time when we stole

something, or went against the rules some way. Then we're
    going to experiment with
        speaking those words with the cello. He's

quiet for a second. *Shiiiiiiiiiiiii....* He gets up and
    leaves by the side door.
        A stone moment is then. You know you will

not be walking back in a high school, despite how cold
    that might sound toward
        young people and our obligations to them,

still there's the turn away from those afternoon
    auditoriums. Your part
        there is done. You may be back in two years

to that very room, but for now it seems through. *You do
    yo own petty theft and play
        it on dee cello. I put yo cello in dee wello.*

The stone fits finely in the dug-out clay. I tamp loose
    topsoil for edging
        and sow the walk with tiny thyme.

Lame Strangers

"Lame but not blind," says an old white man to the
    not quite, I'd guess, so
        old black woman. They're passing

each other in the airport, he with a silver walker,
    she with a green cane,
        "Noooooooooo, not missin' a lick."

The Only News

The hostess at a dinner party in the 1970's took
    my hand in hers at the
        door as I was leaving and pressed the back

of my hand into where on her lower stomach her legs
    meet her torso, that holy
        longed-for cove where we enter this world

like a spaceship opening in Montana. I was very
    excited and not at all
        inclined to bring her before authorities.

We spent some of the next day unsuccessfully on
    the phone trying to
        find a time and place to meet.

Lard Gourd

In the 19th century in Georgia there was a clever
   dog who found he could
      secretly dig his way under the foundations

into the back of a meathouse. The meat was hung
   to smoke too high for his
      leap, but there were gourds loaded with lard

nearer his level. The night he made his entry was
   early in the century.
      The new residents of the land were intruders

themselves, scared and cruel, so when they heard the
   banging about, they did not
      investigate until morning. The dog had

gotten his head stuck in a lard gourd. He couldn't
   see, and he had almost
      smothered out there in the helpless percussion

of his night. This ancient local color allegorizes
   three of my troubling
      conditions: blind desire, panic, and blackout

drinking. I have felt at times that I might be carrying
   the living thread that
      connects the sufi and zen currents, also the

vedantic and high mountain shaman. Then I get drunk,
   talk trash to a sweet saint
      woman, fall out my top bunk, scare the children,

pee indoors, and I know that the golden thread I hold is
   pissant bad behavior and
      not being present for the events of my life.

I am a bad dog with sex and alcohol. I do not lead a pure
   life. Then I remember
      the dog inside his lard inside his gourd inside

himself, the dog that grows still and quiet. I have
    somehow achieved these
        breathing holes, I can't see where I'm going,

but I can breathe. Others have died on nights like this.
    Maybe some human type
        will find me and ungourd my head and scrape

this shit off and groom my face with turpentine. I
    fall on my knees to
        beg forgiveness for meathouse-rude intoxication

and give all praise to the being that lives and watches
    out, dog or not, from
        the gummed-together eyes of the lard gourd dog.

For those not of a monkish cast, I'll explicate: the
    lard is the mind, the
        gourd the container of that, the meathouse this

temptatious world. The dog is me. What gets quiet behind
    the dog's eyes, survives
        and looks out, has no name, except maybe *you.*

The Railing

A child stood on his seat in a restaurant, holding
    to the railing of the chairback
        as though to address a courtroom, "Nobody knows

what's going to happen next!" Then his turning-slide
    back down to his food,
        relieved and proud to say the truth,

as were we to hear it.

What We Learn from Literature

FOR CLINTON AND THE MEDIA

Bill, tell us what we all know: sex is a holy joy, you
    at 50, she at 23, in the
        erotic cloud of Friday night, gentle genital

touch, lips on glans and lips on lips, drinking the clear.
    Henry Miller, Whitman, D.H.
        Lawrence, Galway Kinnell, Edna St.Vincent Millay,

remember these saints of American honesty, gone French,
    gone the Indian subcontinent's
        tantric way, who ask us to say our trance-truth,

as we go into Faulkner's *no-time* kamasutra of the late-night
    office. It's been so long.
        I want this always. You are so dear. You make me

want to scream but I know we can't. When will we be brave
    and live like Gabriel
        Garcia-Marquez in the glee of orgasmic caterwauling?

Instead, this *Scarlet Letter* Dimmesdale, who stands on the
    scaffold pretending to be
        forthright, with lipstick allegations written

all over the tube, when he could be singing, I've got honey
    in my heart and a barrel
        more besides. Plus I'm in the illustrious line

of fucking presidents, William Jefferson Kennedy Roosevelt
    Johnson Clinton, with here
        his saxophone kicking in and a sweetie chorus

doowhopping their obvious delight, and the big A turns
    angelic crimson with gold
        threads and green on a screen as tall

as Chimney Rock of thinnest neoprene.

The Sow and St.Francis

(Galway has the Christian saint bless the pagan
mother as a sow with her litter. Now the goddess
blesses the celibate monk as a sexually repressed
boy-man bachelor. She's devouring his brown
robe as he washes in a stream.)

I bless your body too by chewing this guilt-soaked sweatcloth.
　　Bless your bleached and pubic
　　　　hard-on in the creekpool; soap and rinse, rub dry;

touch whoever and however you wish, Francis. You may fuck
　　yourself silly, dear drop of
　　　　grainy milk. These Egyptian sky-titties rain praise

on your late-afternoon surprise at how my pagan tongue adores
　　your condescension. Adorns.
　　　　Come, and come drift inside the moss-fibrous

limbic lift: my family and I dance in your arms and thighs
　　whether you sit or lay
　　　　drowning in the matin-angelus, freshfrashfranch

branchbriowhiowhawha wheeewhoooowhshwhshwhshwhsh big
　　breath blessing you inside
　　　　me, toes and elegant shin, kin to chin, similar feel,

ribcage, wrist and collarbone, *swich courteseyie, to bend'n
　　nama parts o' me ah ah*
　　　　I hold a smooth ring round your collegial wand,

done-down the blaze of belly hairline, donkey hoof ticking
　　a canyon cliff, sure abut
　　　　the precipice, press a, now's a, please

we dismount and sing a song that rives halfway, old
　　riverbrake cane
　　　　in our mouth, sweet eff, elf.

These Very Feet

A spring stars-just-out nine-thirty when I was five,
    or four, before school,
        that fear, before clothes, I step out of my

bath, am held in the big towel, then leap out to the front
    porch and through the screen
        door, along the curve of boxwood, through

the tower, down its flight of three steps, next flight next
    and next to the open ocean
        of the quadrangle. It doesn't seem like I'm

running, rather more a thought sails into night, the idea
    of nakedness and Blakean
        joy, with my parents and older brother close in

pursuit laughing and finally reaching and snaring the fleeing
    figure back to pajamas and
        bedroom, but these fleet, insouciant feet remember

nothing of that. They became evening air and a bit of sky
    calmly taking another kind
        of bath, with no telling how began their

adoration of moss in the cool brick walk.

The Look on the Dog's Face

How is it dogs know already the big circling
        game they play with
                boys, where the kid and the dog both get

down with forearms along the ground like sphinxes?
        Then the boy runs at
                the dog, and the dog takes off in a circle

that brings it back close enough to be touched but
        not grabbed, and changes
                tack to make a figure-eight out the other

way with the boy in the hourglass door. The game
        needs a lot of space
                for the dog to do right, a field, or

a biggish backyard, though I've seen it done on a
        steep hillside. The look
                on the dog's face is a tricky and

barely embodiable joy.

A Couple

I wish I could draw the picture I saw going by
    me last Thursday
        twilight. A man dressed neatly in pale

colors standing in the grass holding on leash a big
    white short-haired dog,
        who is curled into a C standing with all

four legs in a bunch waiting for defecation to be
    over, the long turd
        stretching to just above the ground

before being deftly pinched off to a proper length.
    I would line-draw
        the scene with strokes of my basting

brush dipped in the pot of India ink on the large
    expanse of drawing
        paper I have stashed. Wonder could I make

it so I wouldn't have to say what it was: solemn,
    sweet, hilarious linkage: a
        dapper, social, patient, calligraphic,

vague, pendant, portentous, amicable couple.

Hopeful

The way people pull into a slanted parking spot at
    the supermarket and leave
        the motor running to keep singing the song we

cannot hear means they have a little extra time, or
    they have been stuck
        in some debilitating routine for twenty-seven

years, and now for no reason it lets them not care
    they're already forty-five
        minutes late. Spread out on the floor upstairs

listening to some semi-classical slosh, they come down
    saying to someone they
        think is there but who's actually not,

I didn't know I liked semi-classical.

The Harp

When it worms and squirms, filling children to
    their tips with the rain
        that washes the funniness of everybody going

about their busyness: a man unfolding a newspaper, a
    woman stepping on an
        automatic grocery store doormat, a teacher

doing algebra on the blackboard. This laughing is
    the best there is; we
        kneel when we hear it. Cole, just beginning

to talk, comes seriously up the basement steps from down
    where his brother Benjamin
        is hammering something, a flat plywoody

bam-bam sound, says to the kitchen adults, "Harold is
    making a harp."

Grace

There's an eruptive quality on mother's side.
    One Thanksgiving my
        cousin Tom Lamar was asked to say grace,

which was a joke since Tom was way too religious for
    church and so began,
        "May the big pumpkin eat the little pumpkin and

all the buzzards left of the river descend to the leafball
    nest in the willow tree
        where sparrow lice are waiting for the squirrel

to return, praise be." Aunt Edith adds quietly, "Thankyee
    Jesus," and everyone sits
        down deadpan till Sally's small one, Mary,

says, "Can I open my eyes now?"

Belden

One job was nightwork, burning a dump, summer
    1956. I had volunteered,
        needing time away from the barrack, the

four of us there in the Forest Service, an ex-Marine
    training college boys to
        build line, how to work the pumps on

the truck, clean campgrounds, and burn the Belden
    dump. He lit it with
        kerosene and left. I sat up to watch

it glow and catch and sail sparks over the Feather
    River, stirring with a
        long iron rod to keep it moving through

the mass. Spot fires were the danger and why I had
    to be there, napping
        on the truck seat, down a lane beside the

post office and bar, which was all there was of
    Belden. Light came, full
        morning, I was exhausted and homesick, as now.

Service

When the way you propose to serve others delights
    you, the doing of it
        brings in some, though very little,

money, keeps you somewhat absorbed in the so-called
    facts of your existence,
        and causes applause, when you almost disappear

inside it, and if others seem nourished in the outcome,
    shall we call that
        serving, O fox, O hummingbird?

Intervals

Every five or seven years I take a hacksaw
    and reach in through
        the giant hydrangea to cut the various

juicy wisteria cords that have begun strapping the
    noble cedar again. Water
        oaks handle whole pirate sail riggings

of purple a lifetime, but the cedar like my soul
    the children climb in
        and make secret rooms at the foot of

must be freed at intervals.

At a Benefit for Rwandan Relief

We ignore the terrible harm we've done. What I know about
    Rwanda is a sunset dust volcanic
        crust cindery-sharp to feet and impossible to

get water from: the hurt in everyone's eyes, cholera and
    parasites and flu and knives. Aggressive
        in some old American polite way it is, to eat lunch

and run errands, dry cleaning and Kinko's. Does Tanzania
    refuse refugees to keep tourism?
        I sit in my paperback cave lined with dream notebooks.

Politics and churches, Israeli field hospitals and Harry
    Belafonte down from Unicef, but
        no loving's quick enough for those now lying down.

What energy wants to murder the already prone? It's not just
    the cruelty of logistics. I leave
        the ivory hut of my skull to take some blame for how

we tribalize the soul, infecting Africa with cleptocracy.
    We steal and divide the presence everyone
        shares through the eyes, where we are alone in

the midst of great beauty. Spiritual jargon, I can stand
    that, or its material loading dock
        absence, either way. I walk to this communal

attempt at relief and will return to my strange room trying
    to get the phone before the
        machine. The cardinal I call George Patton

flies threateningly against his reflection on the glass door.
    We may someday imagine a reliable
        kindness and be, or pretend to be, what

we say we are in the singing.

Nothing

You said after, "That's like the box I went to
    sleep in as a child,
        totally dark and seamlessly

enclosed—not a real box, a way I thought of
    to go to sleep. It had
        no sides, like space. I was falling,

not *from* somewhere *to* somwhere, I just *was*
    free-fall, which is close
        to how it feels to be me. Thank you."

The Art of the Turkish Street Potato

Take a baked potato. Slit it lengthwise. Scoop
    the innards of one side
        into the other, along with the contents

of another whole baked potato. Pour in lots of salt,
    a bunch of butter. Mash
        these around with grated mozzarella and bits

of little hotdogs. Make all a level layer. Add
    tablespoons of mayonnaise
        salad with chunks of chicken. Egg salad

with clouds of papikra. Incorporate and flatten. Now
    Russian salad with beets
        and pieces of green olive and black olive.

Catsuplop. Catsublob. Turn and mesh. Pat the mound
    smooth and set a plastic spoon
        like a gravedigger's spade in the side of

the fresh cemetery plot you have made. Say "Two dollars."
    There is only one immutable rule.
        If you tear the original skin, start over.

The Bus from Yalova to Bursa

We saw three shepherds on the way from Yalova to
　　Bursa. The first, with a large
　　　　flock down meadow, a hundred yards from where

he slept in the tall grass, his dog ten yards away,
　　black and white, sleeping
　　　　as well. Peacefulness posing as drowsy. The

second, a nervous man with four sheep in a tightly
　　compacted figure, heads
　　　　together, he doing the talking. The third had

one confused animal on a leash. The two seemed uncertain
　　who was going someplace. Then
　　　　olive orchards, grey-green leaves in May out

the window, grey-brown trunks, and in between the lines
　　of trees over steep and rocky
　　　　terrain, poppies, a yellow flower, and patches

of heather—lavender, bright scarlet, deep lemon, beneath
　　shades of olive. The flowers
　　　　planted to keep the alleys low and clear for ease

of harvest. Taste one black olive from last year, colors
　　in the brine, old limbs and comic
　　　　shepherds, wet pulp, rock-like seed, more center

than anyone needs. Feel the stone free on your tongue,
　　sliding the rim of cliff like
　　　　a bus full of lovers and memoribilia, bus-o-

bilia! Bus-a-mo, bus-amo-mucho. Dada I'm near you,
　　dadadada lo-ooove divine.

Smoked Cigarette

I am Cecilee Tattybouette, and this is as drunk
    as I get. You may tickle
        my feets with Caribbean beats, but you'll not

give me much to regret. I am Cecilee Tattybouette,
    the one whose agenda is set.
        I don't give a damn if you order the ham;

I'll sit like a smoked cigarette. I am Cecilee
    Tattybouette, and
        this is as drunk as I get.

Namaste for Patrick

At these memorial services I know nothing, and even this I read off a piece of paper. I certainly don't know about planning one's own death. I couldn't do it. Patrick's way seems tremendously brave. Foolish, great-hearted Patrick.

Ever since I partially sponsored the whirling dervishes at the World Congress Center in Atlanta and got a bunch of the old Globe crowd to go, Patrick, whenever he saw me late at night at the Manhattan or riding around in my convertible, he would bow and give the *namaste* hands-together blessing with something poised between mock-piety and pure deep greeting.

It was his way of saying we both know nothing, or exactly as much as the next drunk, which with me was sometimes Patrick when the lights-to-go came harshly on at two-thirty.

The Saint and Sinner Bullshit

A guy with a shaved head, whom I've seen often at the
    Globe, my go for a few beers
        bar late at night, or more, caught me peeing

in the mop sink. I had gone back and forth between
    the two locked bathrooms
        until some compromise was necessary. We

laughed, even though he was who had to mop out the place
    after closing, but what
        is so funny is, the night after he found me

tiptoeing up at the big sink, he was mopping with the very
    mop, while out of the local
        radio came the live culprit, reading mystical

poems as though nothing of the sort.

Dowdy Muse

Dowdy versus sophisticated. Dowdy versus elegant
    and sleek. Frump versus
        runways full of hip-arrogant mincing

bone-girls. Don't let's get masterpiecical.

Half a Peanut Hull

Its many family strew the floorboard of my backseat
    from a session of tossing I
        indulged driving to the mountains one late

afternoon last week. Dints in the hull remember
    the middle ages: armor,
        fatigue, primitively smelted metal, and further

back a baby Canaanite king's coffin, a sideways crooked
    canvas boat, intentionally
        bent, wrung, wronged like this to carry

8th century Irish monks through the surf of the new
    world they would call land
        of the vine. The streaks are columns of ogham,

meanings an Indian dancer opens and offers, fingers
    that never tire. I give
        this spent icon to the man who pushes

a grey plastic barrel on wheels. He smiles for this
    paltriest and recalls
        how lighter-than-air did once hold a sleek nub,

the polished fob of phenomena, thumbshape of Etruscan desire,
    moist and bashful nut. There is
        no sign of where it was ever attached, no navel

for the miraculous missing pea I ate. Is this how body
    flows from spirit and spirit
        from body with no valve? Tendrils flower and lose

flowers, then bend to the ground to perfect their appeal.
    The dull hulls fill beside
        themselves in the earth, until like poetry

bells they lift, dripping dirt and shaking, freed for a
    country dance in the spicy
        town, so within its papery integument the

nut performs a silken hidden hemisphere of taste.

Charlotte Airport Chapel

Five grey chairs and a padded bench to kneel on
    with a Bible open to Mark
        11. A *Qur'an* handy and the Hindu scriptures

we've come to expect, flying. There's an inner door to
    the Chaplain's office. It's
        an 8x10 waiting room, no scheduled worship.

Open 24 hrs., created by Rev. and Mrs, William Zoff, 1992.
    Above, the international symbol
        for holy, an armless kneeling humanoid sacrologo.

This is my kind of stupidity. I will bet on this failure.
    And as I was a little embarrassed
        opening the door, I am a tad so to be caught

leaving the Charlotte International Airport Chapel by a
    security officer, a blonde girl
        wearing a pistol walking by as I exit. O

hopeless little shame room attached to the principal's office,
    I come in here to hear the p.a.
        better. Your attention please Richard Dickweed, meet

your party on the lower level. US Air paging Earthquake Kelly.
    Please, that's *please,* if you would,
        Earthquake Kelly, report to the courtesy counter.

St.Louis passenger Eeeennndeeeweenawemmawoe and Mrs.
    Eeeeeedeeeee pick up the nearest
        red telephone. Exactly like this uncanny nowhere

cubicle there are invisible voices permeating the solid piped-in
musak jet-engined Carly Simon
Loving you's the right thing to do sunset, eeeeeeahhhh

hhyyyyyyynnnnneeeeeyyyhh I change planes through the humming
Charlotte airport once a month,
more and more entering this colorless ham-operated

hermit cell, to kneel by the Downhome Cookin cafeteria.

Fine Arts Auditorium

FOR BILL STAFFORD

Between your four o'clock afternoon poetry reading
　　and dinner at a Chinese-Jewish
　　　　deli called Chow Goldberg, we stopped here, my

house. You said you like to see where poets live. Lots
　　of uh-huh and looking down
　　　　the basement steps and along the bookshelves.

As we stood in the kitchen having a glass of water, you took
　　the steel wool and Comet and poured
　　　　some of your water over the top of my stove. Slowly

the burner rims grew chromy again. After supper we went to a
　　student dance concert. You went
　　　　justifiably to sleep, and when you saw me mock-

reproachfully looking as you jogged awake, you did that
　　downturned mouth-shrug and little
　　　　headback motion I don't know where we all got.

My father did it. Stan Laurel, somebody, taught it to us.
　　You broke open your tickled face
　　　　with the wise Mongolian eyes, and I whispered, "This

would be a nice place for a dance." You got solemn and nodded,
　　sort of head-tilted, then let the silent
　　　　laughing loose anyone could learn from to end up with.

Vent

Last night's dream was a current air-pulse coming
    out a vent: the family
        hilariously turning to particles, a breeze

of ancestors in a windowless hallway. I was feeling
    in the laughter that I
        hadn't lived my center completely

and that I'd have to go back and do it some more.

Night Train, Southern France

Stacks of couchettes sliding sideways to Toulouse,
    we two lying awake on
        top bunks across from each other, writing in

journals with penlights, washed in dream-drumming,
    absurdly happy, splendidly
        silent. A love-ache guides this school of narrow

beds arcing like strands of sound through a longhouse
    silver flute. Your full
        eyes looking at me and now in the dark asleep,

little stations. Between us before dawn, the face of a thief
    intent, fingers probing our
        baggage for stashed wallets and cameras. My eyes

open into his. But now it must be explained how we are
    on the way to meet Jean-Louis
        Stahl, museum curator in Toulouse who will get us

into caves that are normally forbidden. I love the Magdalenian.
    Pretending then, this dark
        Portuguese dock worker, cruel and quick and young,

arm gone to the bicep in our luggage, to have mistaken this
    compartment for another, says
        to me, "Jean-Louis?" From a dim unraveling I reply,

"Stahl?" Which can mean in European languages, "a pretext for
    clandestine activity," or
        "stealing?" It throws him off script. Hermes gives

a material glance, peek at the cooking, catch you later,
    money-quarrels in the morning.
        Light and the jagged laugh of our four German masseuse

suitemates understand the incident in ways concealed from us:
    man and woman, reclining nudes
        on continuous loan, slipping toward a sanctuary of

overlapping animals, as the other we are runs thieving through
    the train, misidentifying
        occupants, footprints opposite and barely above

the gradually slowing, long-expectant, clatter.

Mountain View Cafe

Driving up, I try the new cafe paired in an old
    house with Cooter's Hair,
        Nails, and Tan. Mountain view, Italian

specials every day. Astonishingly for north Georgia,
    the chalkboard says, *escalope*
        potate. He walks from the kitchen. Could

I see a menu? He says nothing, points to my shoes,
    which have strayed off the rolled
        out plastic leading from doormat to counter.

I back up and wipe my feet too much. *Oh-oh, sorry.* As
    his back returns to the kitchen,
        to his wife I deprive us all of joy, *Coffee*

to go. Sometimes if you don't dance quick, there's no
    dance. *Well finally, you're*
        here. Sorry about my feet. Bad feet!

Sometimes we see as from beyond our bodies a love that
    walks in hungry, foreign,
        muddy-footed, stubborn, customer and cook.

Natural Observation

Sixteen years overlooking this creek, I understand how
    these beavers are mistaken.
        They cannot build a lodge here. It's too

swift, but their instincts think they have! Living
    inside a natural network of
        hollows the underground springs have formed in

the sandy flood-plain I live on top of, they swim out and
    gnaw bark off great tulip
        poplars. The trees die, lean and fall and get

washed downstream, unusable. But the animals ignore the
    ridiculous failure and cling
        to the ruse of maintenance, doing brave riparian

work, because as they slide back in, the muddy honeycomb
    home is still solidly there.
        They could, if they would, hang out inside and not

do one constructive thing. But they will not accept the
    truth of how easy this
        location is. I don't need for any community's

sake to be smoozing the white necks of trees. Let these
    animals wriggle the eddies
        and root-forest edges in full view of my

flashlight. Exercise keeps the building genes strong. And
    we both can rest now
        having thought of another false purpose.

Clothing Swap

I have women friends who gather on an evening every
    three or four months to
        put all sorts of items from their closets and

cabinets—shoes, sweaters, coats, dresses, lipsticks,
    perfume they're tired of—in
        piles around someone's livingroom-dining area.

Then they cruise in their underwear trying on possibles.
    Picture this subversive
        model for a marketplace without capital: a

high-up California house with eight to ten women, thirty to
    any age, as I have said
        in underwear, or naked, sportively arming

and legging on each other's freebie castoffs. Delight
    in finds, communism forgot,
        is what a healthy alertness craves. It makes

everyone shop differently, when they do shop, remembering
    how some skirt will later
        drape Joanne, Maggie, Yofe, Elaine, not just

will it suit, but how they will be made to smile. Now pan
    from pastel panties frisking
        to the mall across about to shrink to a

coffeetable collectible in this revolutionary dance of
    women's ingenuity and glamor
        that men are easily called into with their own

jackets and ties, books and broken lamps. O distribution
    centers in Cincinnati, you
        middle managers who add no patient detail of

exhilaration, you do not handle cloth enough to hold it up
    to the light and you don't
        get any money. If this seems naive and

unworkably potlatchian economics, imagine it happening
in a soul-place where animae
yak and trade wrappings, until we're

sitting here pretty much finished, drinking herbal tea,
talking serious change,
traipsed out in pieces of everybody's gift.

Gauze

I played Joseph once in the Christmas tableau at
    the First Presbyterian
        Church in Chattanooga. Some girl, a

beautiful madonna-sexy older-than-me ninth grader
    was Mary, Amy Somebody.
        We were lit by a baby-glow that the

congregation couldn't see from out in their lower
    dark was a light bulb
        covered with gauze. There began my

stagelife, cuckolded by God, without a speaking
    part, standing with fake
        wise men in pure mystical solitude.

Cloud

Horse torso, Jefferson asleep. Dog's head, lute,
    baby on back, goose!
        Dumbo, dice, blue alligator, balled-up

pages, turned-over turtle, half-drowned barge,
    tilted hay. Melting
        corpse, cows in fog, brassiere, trowel.

Kingsnake

One year he let me touch him moving under the iron
    steps. One year, to
        see his whole body beneath the trilliums.

Now he's left a six-foot skin across my stone threshold.
    The great changing we
        give comes as we slough winter and glide

like summer's low-roof diamond-floor of invisible skin.

Driving Back from the Mountains

Sun leaving in the rearview mid-October. Goodbye
    gorgeous air. Goodbye
        shutdown ice cream store with your sign

saying only REAM, goodbye leaf-traffic, goodbye
    Hairport 53, goodbye
        boat storage sheds. Goodbye serious

concerns, goodbye prayer. So long song, riding along
    with barely a sound. Maybe
        not goodbye telepathy. Hello full telepathy.

Sunset has a little more to do. You would not say
    it's night yet, not the
        feel of that, though death is in the car,

sitting in the backseat, distracted out the window,
    nothing particular, hat
        tilted on his head like my father in the late

afternoon of the 1950's. Goodbye four motorcycles on
    a trailer being pulled.
        This feather-tinge was the first image

I ever wrote down, the wake of some dark feather that
    fell just now. Goodbye
        you pale rubbed glow. Goodbye breathing out

lightly the Mispeh benediction, *while we are absent*
    one from the other. Lord
        watch between. Trees more black. Goodbye

doubt, so dear to me and not yet done, between two rows
    of orange barrels narrowing.
        Goodbye dog being patiently given water, patiently

lapping. Goodbye glass of water, the slow huge dew forming
    everywhere. Now in the frontseat
        with me, sky its richest dark darkblue. Goodbye

poetry. Big chunks of excitement fly off in nightair, no
    stars yet. Goodbye holy
        softball halogen towers of Bishop Park. Goodbye

God. *God be w'yee, God.* The Christian fabric shop.
    Goodbye corduroy, threads
        of the king. Never goodbye laughter, never

those I love. The Sunday night driveway tunnels through,
    key, message machine massaging.
        Death intimately inside my forehead, behind

sight, lying on the couch in the dark, with the door
    open and all the stuff
        still out in the car. Goodbye home.

Straying

Prying the nameplate off the office door that's been
    mine since this annex
        was built, slipping a screwdriver under

the glued-on COLEMAN BARKS, I make room for the linguistic
    atlas-maker, drive home
        with the last load of books, and weep. Then

I stop weeping. Country cemeteries say he's gone to his
    rest, this sweet afternoon
        nap, taking off my glasses beside me

on the bed, ears afloat in phenomenal murmur. Last night
    two dogs followed me on my
        hour-walk. They picked up on Springdale,

McWhorter, Cherokee, the way dogs will, walking ahead
    but staying with me no
        matter the complications of the route,

young ones. All I said was, *How you guys doing?*

Elegy for John Seawright

or, *The Improvement of Sensual Enjoyment*

I saw eternity the other night like a great ring
    of pure and endless
        light, all calm as it was bright.

There is an eternity around that looks out and weeps
    from a place behind our
        eyes, where we are grateful, from where

we recognize beauty, where lives a dragon guarding
    unimaginable wealth, and
        giving it away too, prodigal dragon, a

waterfalling darkness in the center of the mountain,
    whatever *gold* means to
        Renaissance alchemists, the fine refining of

self, the river's motion, waterlights sliding on a cliff,
    a walk in the evening, your
        arm lifted to a friend a block away, God on

the porch a thunder and lightning June afternoon, your
    jagged jot and scribble on a
        piece of several-times-folded paper. *I love you,*

man. So we have these feet to put boots on to investigate
    how it goes about the
        building of Jerusalem, this word-weary

soul-world of footprint, footprint, waltz and samba. So
    go on; this is ours to
        finish, or to leave with a lot undone

as you have. There's some other thing you will no doubt
    get good at. Someone turned
        one time in a crowd of tourists leaving

the Cathedral of St.John the Divine in New York City and
    said to me, a perfect stranger,
        "Don't forget to turn out the lights."

The week before John died I was driving through Fivepoints
    intersection and had
        the thought that John was about to change jobs.

I had meant to tease him about it but never did, that
    definite premonition of
        his death. A door opens in the side of a cliff

looking through to a wide empty plain, beautifully bare.
    Behind the door on the other
        side there's a cubbyhole you could crawl

into, but someone says it hasn't worked; the winters are
    too severe this high. One
        must not get cozy in a hideout behind

the death door, tempting niche of grief. I may not be
    where I was when you last
        saw me. I think these be true images,

the crawl-in cave near the wooden door in the side of a
    grey cliff. They came in dream.
        I long for scenes and notions of what lives

and lives through death. How friends continue. Whatever
    makes the taste of a laugh-look,
        the talking so crystalline-passionate,

though unbreathable like the green air inside an emerald.
    A young man is washing glass
        double doors with a windex pump-spray and

a rag. He has broken the middle finger on his right hand.
    It's taped up, grandly enlarged,
        and slightly curved so that despite his calm

demeanor he's in magnificent, constant defiance. We are
glory-bound under a mosque-shaped
potato-cloud. Love those who can hear your fear.

Exuberance *is* beauty, and clear reservations justly put
are also attractive. The road
of excess leads to the palace of wisdom,

but not today. Drive your cart and your plow over the bones
of the dead, and try sometime
to visit the tombs of sufis singing, *La*, singing

La illaha il'Allah Huuuuuuu No major complaint, no minor
insight. The cry of the parrot
is louder than the cry of the turtle.

Age is meaning and meaning is killing us. Blake loves
minute particulars, but he
does not get around to mentioning many,

as Whitman did, spraying the pavement with sparkles off
a knife-grinder's emery
wheel. A very pregnant woman in Kinko's

is carefully making enlargement copies. Find your children
and sit down with them.
Hot pies make cold conversation. Baking

takes precise patience. Nakedness is the work of God.
Lust is the bounty of
God. The laugh of John Seawright is a tickling

light in the flower-throat of a summer late afternoon
glimmering out for
a pointless drive on the vast Athens bypass.

So open the five inlets of soul as lightning bugs come forth
at 17 to 9. What do
they do all day? They down there in the dirt

with they lights off getting work done like the rest of us.
　　　Nightime's for cruising.
　　　　　You know, they think they've found what it is

allows a lightning bug to cut himself on and off. Nitric
　　　oxide, the same chemical
　　　　　that controls heart rate and memory in humans.

Some cell in a lightning bug combines with air to make
　　　nitric oxide, which
　　　　　scientists call NO. At a spontaneous

signal from the lightning bug's brain—consider that—
　　　the NO gets released;
　　　　　adjacent cells shut down: this gives off

a pulse of oxygen which triggers an enzyme that turns on
　　　the light, all in a millisecond
　　　　　says Barry Trimmer, biologist at Tufts.

Sara Lewis, fellow firefly expert, says there are 200
　　　different species with 200
　　　　　different signaling sequences. Lightning bugs

live for two years as larvae in the soil. Then only two
　　　weeks as adults in their
　　　　　14-night courtship phase. Life is intense

and short. *Glow, little glowworm*. It's the males who
　　　send sequences. Females
　　　　　answer, one wink. But this could change

next week when the current lightning will have panned
　　　away. Mark Twain said the
　　　　　adequate word is to the right word as

a lightning bug is to lightning. He's right, but he
　　　hadn't heard a thing about
　　　　　the big NO with its release to YES, as the

folds of time and place circle like a pony at the end of
    a coriolis rope riding the
        horizon in layers of iridescent intelligence.

There is surely more to this flint-rant, pool-umbrella love
    for thunderstorms. Shenanigan
        chiaroscuro, mover-along, a man sits on his

bed with his bare feet on the floor, leaning back all the
    way flat, arms out foot
        to head, one palm east, the other west. This

is such a comfortable posture to listen to the measures
    kindling, others draining
        through gravel: and after that your feet

make no print, nor scatter any pigeon, nor dig one
    heel for purchase, nor
        slide nor dance, and I wait for how to

say the blank forehead, a peeled stick, the hesitant,
    doldrum soul: a pine
        cone with rolled mud for legs. The helpless

terror, the flung note. Two crows walk in smooth sand
    making a single
        sentence, that is also conversation, with

insect-peck punctuation. Now one lifts, then the other,
    into open air again.

A NOTE

Poet, writer, historian, polymath, artist, cook, and friend, John
Seawright, died at age 44 on May 9, 2001, of a brain aneurysm.

Remarks at John Seawright's burial service at the Sunshine Methodist Church near Toccoa, Georgia, May 13, 2001.

I am Coleman Barks. I have a small company called Maypop Books that John ran the day-to-day operation of the last four or five years. We publish mostly Persian mystical poetry.

You all are about the bravest bunch I can imagine. Because you have decided, being of sound mind and willingly of your own accord, to enter a graveyard in northeast Georgia with John Ryan Seawright. You might be here a while.

And since you're here you might start a sentence that begins John Seawright loved..., a sentence that would get you tangled in the very threads of infinity and existence, because John loved so deeply the strands of geneology and family and event and thought that bind us together in our pain and joy, our eccentricity and common glory. He knew and held those strands like the reins of our living, and of our continuously evolving soul he was one of the keepers.

John Seawright loved music. Many can say how that went better than I. The singing, the preposterous serenading house to house in and around Lavonia and Carnesville on Twelfth Night at the turn of the century, was just one of the notes he held.

John Seawright loved *the place,* meaning where his parents live down the road, and too, the three hundred billion, or is it million, galaxies we so casually and forgetfully inhabit. John Seawright with his tremendous heart loved his mama and daddy, his brother Sam, and Cynthia, and so many others. No words of mine can say anything close to what and how he felt.

John Seawright loved memory. John Seawright loved tenderness.

John Seawright did not love television or the cheapening dilution of our spiritual longing, however that occurs. John did not love banana pudding.

John Seawright loved the making we do in concert with the

generosity of the ground, air, and sunlight. He planted a crop of gourds the week before he died because he felt a good rain coming.

What make is that car? What make is this give and take of breathing we do with one another?

John Seawright loved talking and cooking.

John loved asking about cow vetch and white mulberries and the spotted sandpiper and the joy of the moment when identification settles in, he crosses a leg, holds up one finger, and says, *That's it.*

The world of spirit where John is is not so strange. What's truly odd is that we're in these bodies in the Sunshine Church on a Monday afternoon in May 2001. It's very strange and precious and precarious, yet wonderfully important, how we're with each other and continue to talk and laugh and hold forth.

I think John Seawright loved the strangeness and the fragility. But wait a minute. I have no wisdom about what's familiar, then not so familiar anymore. I'm just throwing words at the immensity of his life as it was lived with such love and attention.

Shakespeare with his enlightened kindness slung some better scattershot language at the living mystery. Here's a passage from the end of *King Lear*, one that John loved.

> Come let's away to prison:
> We two alone will sing like birds i' the cage:
> When thou dost ask me blessing, I'll kneel down
> And ask of thee forgiveness: so we'll live,
> And pray, and sing, and tell old tales, and laugh
> At gilded butterflies, and hear poor rogues
> Talk of court news; and we'll talk with them too,
> Who loses and who wins, who's in, who's out;
> And take upon's the mystery of things,
> As though we were God's spies....

> (V,iii,8-17)

John Seawright did take on the mystery of things, and was, for a fact, God's spy.

Right there, right there, with everything he tended to, the sweet small calculations grew.

JOHN SEAWRIGHT'S EPITAPH:

*Love brought me this far by the hand, then
just kept standing there, not letting go.*

(slightly altered from Seamus Heaney's "The Walk" in *The Spirit Level*, Farrar, Straus and Giroux, 1996, p.74)